A Swinger
of Birches

Also in this series
I'M NOBODY! WHO ARE YOU?
Poems of Emily Dickinson for Children
illustrated by Rex Schneider

UNDER THE GREENWOOD TREE
Shakespeare for Young People
illustrated by Patricia and Robin DeWitt

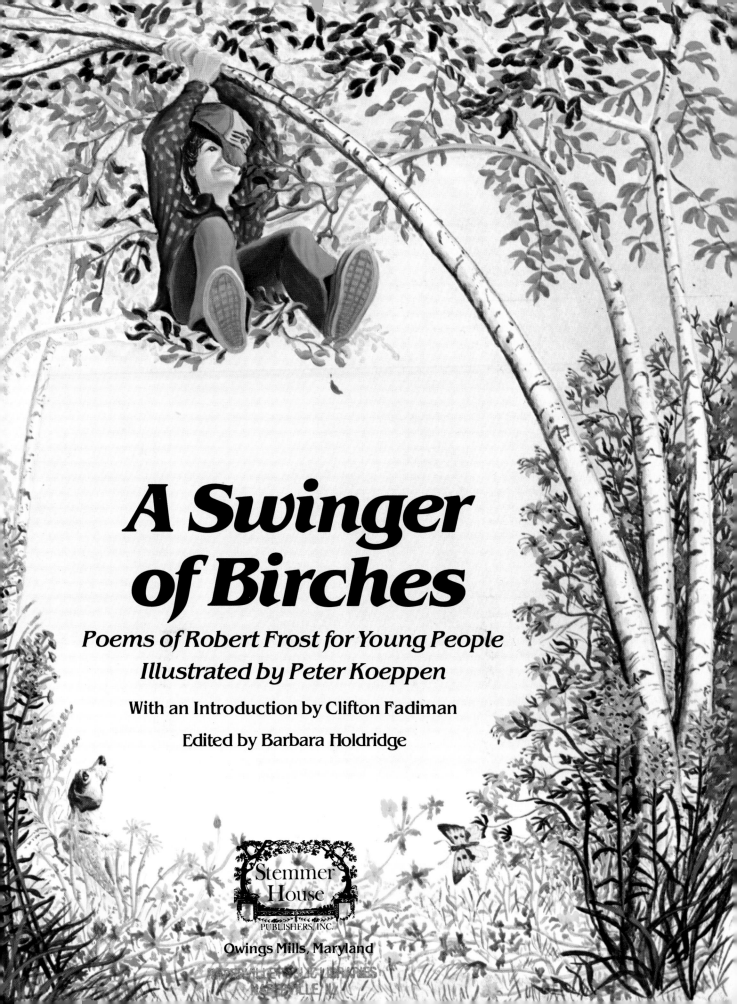

A Swinger of Birches

Poems of Robert Frost for Young People

Illustrated by Peter Koeppen

With an Introduction by Clifton Fadiman

Edited by Barbara Holdridge

Stemmer
House
PUBLISHERS, INC.

Owings Mills, Maryland

Acknowledgment

From THE POETRY OF ROBERT FROST edited by Edward Connery Lathem. Copyright 1916, 1923, 1928, 1934, 1939, 1947, © 1967, 1969 by Holt, Rinehart and Winston. Copyright 1936, 1944, 1951, © 1956, 1962 by Robert Frost. Copyright © 1964, 1975 by Lesley Frost Ballantine. Reprinted by permission of Holt, Rinehart and Winston, Publishers.

Inquiries should be directed to
Stemmer House Publishers, Inc.
2627 Caves Road
Owings Mills, Maryland 21117

A Barbara Holdridge book
Printed and bound in Hong Kong
First printing 1982
Second printing 1984
Third printing 1987
Fourth printing 1990

Library of Congress Cataloging in Publication Data

Frost, Robert, 1874-1963.
    A swinger of birches.

    "A Barbara Holdridge book"—Verso t.p.
    Summary: A selection of thirty-eight poems celebrating the natural and spiritual worlds by the well-loved poet of rural New England.
    1. Children's poetry, American. [1. American poetry] I. Koeppen, Peter, ill. II. Title.
PS3511.R94A6 1982   811'.52   82-5517
ISBN 0-916144-92-5   AACR2
ISBN 0-916144-93-3 (pbk.)

A Swinger of Birches

Contents

Introduction by Clifton Fadiman   9

Birches   18

Nothing Gold Can Stay   22

Spring Pools   23

Hyla Brook   24

Leaves Compared with Flowers   26

In Hardwood Groves   27

A Young Birch   28

Mending Wall   29

The Gift Outright   31

Come In   32

Fireflies in the Garden   34

Devotion   36

A Passing Glimpse   37

One Guess   38

The Oven Bird   39

A Drumlin Woodchuck   40

Departmental   43

Canis Major   46

A Minor Bird   47

The Rose Family   48

The Secret Sits   48

The Pasture   49

The Road Not Taken   50

Gathering Leaves   52

Now Close the Window   54

A Late Walk   55

Acquainted with the Night   56

The Last Word of a Bluebird   58

A Peck of Gold   60

Tree at My Window   62

Questioning Faces   64

Dust of Snow   66

The Runaway   68

Fire and Ice   70

Looking for a Sunset Bird in Winter   72

Stopping by Woods on a Snowy Evening   74

To the Thawing Wind   76

A Patch of Old Snow   77

Glossary   78

Introduction

I.

My slight acquaintance with Robert Frost began years ago in the grand ballroom of the Waldorf-Astoria hotel in New York City. As I shared the platform I had a good chance to observe him as he read his poetry aloud to an attentive audience. After finishing a certain poem—I wish I could recall it, perhaps it is in this very book—he looked at his audience with (I think) a twinkle in his eye. Then, just a mite sternly, he said, "I have a feeling you didn't understand that poem. I'll say it again." And he did.

Notice that he used the word "say"—rather than "read." For Frost, poetry was a special kind of *talk*. He wanted to make you hear a real voice behind every line. *His* voice, of course, not an ordinary voice. He wanted you to hear its tone, its little hesitations, its breaks and pauses.

Let me give you an example. One of his finest poems is called "The Death of the Hired Man." It's too long to put in this book. At a certain point one of the people in the poem says,

> Home is the place where, when you have to go there,
> They have to take you in.

Try reading it aloud, "with expression," as they say. You can't do it. You're forced, by the way the words are arranged, to "talk" it. You have to pause a little after "where" and "there" as if you weren't quite sure how to say what's in your mind. It sounds like someone thinking out loud—precisely what Frost intended. Notice also how simple the language is. Every word is just one syllable, and they're all words we knew when we were three years old. But the feeling carried by the words isn't simple at all. They make us stop and think. Then we say, "Yes, that's true. That's what a home is. I never would have put it that way. But it's just right—and it *sounds* right."

Perhaps you can see now why Robert Frost "said" his poems.

Sometimes we think of poets as dreamers, far away from "real life." That's not true of good poets. I observed Frost's face as he sat beside me on the platform. He looked like a shrewd, intelligent farmer, one who had worked and thought a lot. It was a craggy face, seamed, open-airish, topped with a shock of fine white hair. His eyes seemed to be looking in at his own thought and yet also looking out, measuring his audience. Not a dreamy face at all.

Ask your parents whether they remember watching on television the inauguration of John F. Kennedy on a cold January day in 1961. If they do they may also remember Robert Frost stepping forward to say a poem, preceding the swearing-in of the President. He was then 87, only two years away from death. He was bent, gnarled like an old tree, chilled by the cutting wind. And then we all noticed that the sun was in his eyes—and very old, failing eyes they were. He fumbled with his manuscript. President-to-be Kennedy tried to help him, but it was no use. He uttered a few words, stopped. Tens of millions of Americans watched in agonized sympathy, knowing that this public moment was also one of the greatest in the old poet's long life. At last Robert Frost drew himself together and very quietly announced that he would ``say'' another poem. Then with great dignity he recited from memory ``The Gift Outright,'' which you will find on page 31, and which was perfectly adapted to the solemn occasion. No one watching the white-haired ancient poet handle that critical situation will forget him.

Nor, by the way, should they forget that John Kennedy was one of only two Presidents in our century (the other was Theodore Roosevelt) who have recognized how much poets contribute to the real greatness of any country.

II

Robert Frost looked and spoke like a New Englander but was actually born in San Francisco, in 1874. When he was eleven his father died and his mother took Robert and his sister to Lawrence, Massachusetts. The family was poor, supported by Mrs. Frost's schoolteaching. At his high-school graduation Robert Frost was co-valedictorian, along with a pretty girl named Elinor Miriam White. He later married her. It's interesting that the year before their marriage he published his first book, *Twilight*. ``Published'' is not the right word. It contained only six poems and the entire edition consisted of two copies, one for himself and one for his sweetheart.

Even as a boy Robert was determined to be a poet. His grandfather destined him for the law and sent him to Dartmouth College in New Hampshire. But Frost dropped out before finishing even his first term. Living at home he tried schoolteaching, newspaper reporting, and other jobs. But he kept on with his verse, which found little or no market. In 1897—by this time he was married—he entered Harvard. But after less than two years he dropped out again, because of illness. In Derry, New Hampshire he tried poultry-farming; his neighbors

11

called him "the egg man." He failed, turned once more to teaching, did little better at that, sold his farm, and in 1912 took his family (there were now several children) with him to England.

This was a daring thing to do, for they had little money and no prospects. But Robert Frost was a stubborn man who knew his own mind and made his family bend to his will. Great poets are often like that. Something in them, their genius, demands to be let out and will not allow circumstances or other people to stand in the way. So it was with Frost. The family had to live modestly in a little country cottage, while Frost labored over his poems and made literary friends who were to be useful to him later on.

His career is unusual for an American. He was recognized not in his own country but in England, where his first two books were published to much praise. When the first of these came out he was almost forty, an age at which most men would hardly think of starting a career.

In 1915 the Frosts returned to New Hampshire. Robert bought a small farm and they settled down. But he was never much of a farmer, even though many of his poems are about the lives of isolated country people or about their natural surroundings. He used to say that he was too lazy to farm. Because he liked to read and write poetry late into the night he changed his cow's milking schedule, milking her at midnight and noon. We don't know what the cow thought of this, but it allowed Frost to keep poets' rather than farmers' hours. We shouldn't take too seriously Frost's statement that he was lazy. It's hard to prove but I'm convinced that it takes far more emotional and mental energy to write fine poetry than to run General Motors.

From this time on his worth was recognized by his own countrymen. He became ever more popular and successful, extending his influence on young people through various teaching jobs at important colleges. In 1963, at the great age of 89, he died, laden with honors and secure in the knowledge that his name and life work were familiar even to small children. There is a mountain in Vermont named after him. But to keep his memory green no mountain is needed.

III.

Each poet has his own special notion of what poetry is. Robert Frost once called it "a momentary stay against confusion." What does that mean? Well, life is bewildering to all of us, especially if we have alert minds and can feel things and think about them, instead of just letting them happen. A poem—at least Frost's kind of poem—sorts out some of this bewilderment and for a moment makes something clear—an experience, a remembered scene, the relationship of father and child, whatever the poem may be about.

Frost also once said that a poem "begins in delight and ends in wisdom." What does that mean? There has to be first a kind of excitement as an idea flashes or floats or slides into the poet's mind. Or it may not be an idea. It may be a picture or a stray line or even a couple of words. Gradually the poem develops out of the idea or picture or phrase. When it's finished, the poet should have said something about human beings or the natural world that adds to our sense of what living is all about. I think that is what Frost means first by "delight," then by "wisdom."

Let's look at a few poems together. That might help us understand Frost's feelings about what he devoted his long life to.

"The Pasture" (page 49) is almost surely addressed to one of his children. If you read it quickly it doesn't seem to be saying much beyond an invitation to the child to come watch the poet clean a spring and fetch a calf. But if this were all, it wouldn't be a favorite poem, beloved by millions of people. It gives us two sharp pictures: the spring and the little tottering calf. The pictures make us at once feel the quality of farm life. They give us, to use Frost's word, "delight." But the poem is not really about the spring and the calf. What it's about lies in the terribly simple words, "You come too." The poem is about a father and a child loving each other and sharing an experience together. That may be its "wisdom." Perhaps we feel way down deep that the little calf and the small unnamed child have something in common. Now read it aloud. It sounds like a real person talking. And Frost does all this in eight lines, using the simplest words. Good poetry is the *shortest* way of saying something complicated. It's economical.

That is, it does a great deal of work on our minds and on our feelings without wasting words. To show how true this is, read the very paragraph I have just written. It has taken me many, many words to "explain" the poem. But the poem, if we read it with attention, explains itself much better and more quickly than I have done. Nevertheless, sometimes talking *about* a poem can help us identify more closely what it has to give us.

A certain French poet named Mallarmé wrote very differently from Frost. But he once said something with which Frost would agree. He said that to *name* an object is to take away three-fourths of the pleasure. "To *suggest* it, that is the ideal." In "The Pasture" we've seen how much is suggested.

This is even truer of one of Frost's most famous poems, "The Road Not Taken" (page 50). It seems to be about a real experience. The poet comes upon two diverging roads and chooses one rather than the other. But what Frost "names" (the actual roads in the yellow wood) is unimportant compared to what he suggests. And what he suggests, in only twenty lines, is really the whole of human life. In a way life does consist of making millions of small and sometimes large choices. The wrong choice—or, indeed, the right one—can make "all the difference." The poem is also (see the last stanza) about remembering one's youth, remembering it, as we tend to do, with sadness, "with a sigh." Much more is suggested than said directly. In other words, the poet cunningly arranges his words so that *we* feel what he had in mind. In this sense he does part of the job, and our imaginations finish it. A kind of division of labor.

It is a mistake to think that poets write only about lovely things. They are only incidentally interested in beauty. What they are really interested in is power—the power of their words to make us feel, see, dream, think, be astonished.

Sometimes the mood is dark and bitter, but bitterness can be interesting. Look at "Fire and Ice" (page 70). The *form* of the poem (its rhyme scheme, its use of several abrupt short lines) is in its way beautiful. But what it says, about the end of the world and about human desire and human hate, is chilling. Poets are not always kindly and loving and do not always write about flowers and springtime.

Perhaps Frost's most famous poem is "Stopping by Woods on a Snowy Evening." Everyone loves it, everyone is moved by it, but it may say a different thing to each of us. It is one of his most "mysterious" poems, and it is the mystery that grips us, as well as the simple but carefully composed *music* of the lines themselves. As with "The Road Not Taken" it seems to be talking not about woods and snow and a little horse but about life. Wonderful moments ("The woods are lovely, dark and deep") come to all of us. But we cannot stay with them. We must keep our promises to others, we must press on and meet whatever experiences await us, before the end comes, whether we call it sleep or death. This poem has the supreme quality of magic, something we can't explain. Part of the magic lies in the repetition of "And miles to go before I sleep" at the end. Try reading the stanza leaving out the very last line. Feel how much is lost. Can you figure out why?

Some of the poems in this book require very thoughtful reading, even several readings. One example is "Birches" (page 18). As with much of Frost's work, we at first like it because it brings us close to a lovely object in nature, in this case a birch tree. Then we get a sense of how it feels to a boy to swing on the tree. Finally the real meaning of the poem, which has been there all the time, gradually emerges. "Birches" turns out to be about the fun of swinging on a birch tree. But it is also about the joys of living here on earth and the feeling one gets occasionally that there are higher joys to be found in aspiring "toward heaven." Perhaps we need to have both feelings: "One could do worse than be a swinger of birches."

Santa Barbara, California   Clifton Fadiman
April 1982

A Swinger
of Birches

BIRCHES

When I see birches bend to left and right
Across the lines of straighter darker trees,
I like to think some boy's been swinging them.
But swinging doesn't bend them down to stay
As ice storms do. Often you must have seen them
Loaded with ice a sunny winter morning
After a rain. They click upon themselves
As the breeze rises, and turn many-colored
As the stir cracks and crazes their enamel.
Soon the sun's warmth makes them shed crystal shells
Shattering and avalanching on the snow crust—
Such heaps of broken glass to sweep away
You'd think the inner dome of heaven had fallen.
They are dragged to the withered bracken by the load,
And they seem not to break; though once they are bowed
So low for long, they never right themselves:
You may see their trunks arching in the woods
Years afterwards, trailing their leaves on the ground
Like girls on hands and knees that throw their hair
Before them over their heads to dry in the sun.

But I was going to say when Truth broke in
With all her matter-of-fact about the ice-storm
I should prefer to have some boy bend them
As he went out and in to fetch the cows—
Some boy too far from town to learn baseball,
Whose only play was what he found himself,
Summer or winter, and could play alone.
One by one he subdued his father's trees
By riding them down over and over again
Until he took the stiffness out of them,
And not one but hung limp, not one was left
For him to conquer. He learned all there was
To learn about not launching out too soon
And so not carrying the tree away
Clear to the ground. He always kept his poise
To the top branches, climbing carefully
With the same pains you use to fill a cup
Up to the brim, and even above the brim.
Then he flung outward, feet first, with a swish,
Kicking his way down through the air to the ground.

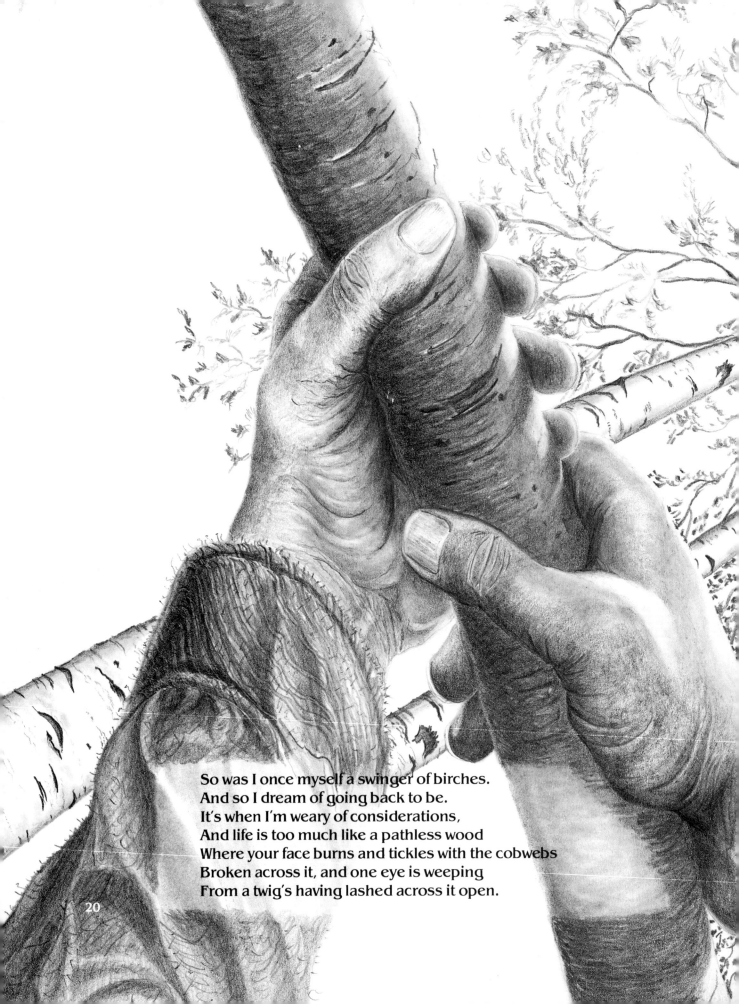

So was I once myself a swinger of birches.
And so I dream of going back to be.
It's when I'm weary of considerations,
And life is too much like a pathless wood
Where your face burns and tickles with the cobwebs
Broken across it, and one eye is weeping
From a twig's having lashed across it open.

20

I'd like to get away from earth awhile
And then come back to it and begin over.
May no fate willfully misunderstand me
And half grant what I wish and snatch me away
Not to return. Earth's the right place for love:
I don't know where it's likely to go better.
I'd like to go by climbing a birch tree,
And climb black branches up a snow-white trunk
Toward heaven, till the tree could bear no more,
But dipped its top and set me down again.
That would be good both going and coming back.
One could do worse than be a swinger of birches.

NOTHING GOLD CAN STAY

Nature's first green is gold,
Her hardest hue to hold.
Her early leaf's a flower;
But only so an hour.
Then leaf subsides to leaf.
So Eden sank to grief,
So dawn goes down to day.
Nothing gold can stay.

22

SPRING POOLS

These pools that, though in forests, still reflect
The total sky almost without defect,
And like the flowers beside them, chill and shiver,
Will like the flowers beside them soon be gone,
And yet not out by any brook or river,
But up by roots to bring dark foliage on.

The trees that have it in their pent-up buds
To darken nature and be summer woods—
Let them think twice before they use their powers
To blot out and drink up and sweep away
These flowery waters and these watery flowers
From snow that melted only yesterday.

HYLA BROOK

By June our brook's run out of song and speed.
Sought for much after that, it will be found
Either to have gone groping underground
(And taken with it all the Hyla breed
That shouted in the mist a month ago,
Like ghost of sleigh-bells in a ghost of snow)—
Or flourished and come up in jewel-weed,
Weak foliage that is blown upon and bent
Even against the way its waters went.
Its bed is left a faded paper sheet
Of dead leaves stuck together by the heat—
A brook to none but who remember long.
This as it will be seen is other far
Than with brooks taken otherwhere in song.
We love the things we love for what they are.

LEAVES COMPARED WITH FLOWERS

A tree's leaves may be ever so good,
So may its bark, so may its wood;
But unless you put the right thing to its root
It never will show much flower or fruit.

But I may be one who does not care
Ever to have tree bloom or bear.
Leaves for smooth and bark for rough,
Leaves and bark may be tree enough.

Some giant trees have bloom so small
They might as well have none at all.
Late in life I have come on fern.
Now lichens are due to have their turn.

I bade men tell me which in brief,
Which is fairer, flower or leaf.
They did not have the wit to say,
Leaves by night and flowers by day.

Leaves and bark, leaves and bark,
To lean against and hear in the dark.
Petals I may have once pursued.
Leaves are all my darker mood.

IN HARDWOOD GROVES

The same leaves over and over again!
They fall from giving shade above
To make one texture of faded brown
And fit the earth like a leather glove.

Before the leaves can mount again
To fill the trees with another shade,
They must go down past things coming up,
They must go down into the dark decayed.

They *must* be pierced by flowers and put
Beneath the feet of dancing flowers.
However it is in some other world
I know that this is the way in ours.

27

A YOUNG BIRCH

The birch begins to crack its outer sheath
Of baby green and show the white beneath,
As whosoever likes the young and slight
May well have noticed. Soon entirely white
To double day and cut in half the dark
It will stand forth, entirely white in bark,
And nothing but the top a leafy green—
The only native tree that dares to lean,
Relying on its beauty, to the air.
(Less brave perhaps than trusting are the fair.)
And someone reminiscent will recall
How once in cutting brush along the wall
He spared it from the number of the slain,
At first to be no bigger than a cane,
And then no bigger than a fishing pole,
But now at last so obvious a bole
The most efficient help you ever hired
Would know that it was there to be admired,
And zeal would not be thanked that cut it down
When you were reading books or out of town.
It was a thing of beauty and was sent
To live its life out as an ornament.

28

MENDING WALL

Something there is that doesn't love a wall,
That sends the frozen-ground-swell under it
And spills the upper boulders in the sun,
And makes gaps even two can pass abreast.
The work of hunters is another thing:
I have come after them and made repair
Where they have left not one stone on a stone,
But they would have the rabbit out of hiding,
To please the yelping dogs. The gaps I mean,
No one has seen them made or heard them made,
But at spring mending-time we find them there.
I let my neighbor know beyond the hill;
And on a day we meet to walk the line
And set the wall between us once again.
We keep the wall betwen us as we go.
To each the boulders that have fallen to each.
And some are loaves and some so nearly balls
We have to use a spell to make them balance:
"Stay where you are until our backs are turned!"
We wear our fingers rough with handling them.
Oh, just another kind of outdoor game,
One on a side. It comes to little more:
There where it is we do not need the wall:

29

He is all pine and I am apple orchard.
My apple trees will never get across
And eat the cones under his pines, I tell him.
He only says, "Good fences make good neighbors."
Spring is the mischief in me, and I wonder
If I could put a notion in his head:
"*Why* do they make good neighbors? Isn't it
Where there are cows? But here there are no cows.
Before I built a wall I'd ask to know
What I was walling in or walling out,
And to whom I was like to give offense.
Something there is that doesn't love a wall,
That wants it down." I could say "Elves" to him,
But it's not elves exactly, and I'd rather
He said it for himself. I see him there,
Bringing a stone grasped firmly by the top
In each hand, like an old stone savage armed.
He moves in darkness as it seems to me,
Not of woods only and the shade of trees.
He will not go behind his father's saying,
And he likes having thought of it so well
He says again, "Good fences make good neighbors."

THE GIFT OUTRIGHT

The land was ours before we were the land's.
She was our land more than a hundred years
Before we were her people. She was ours
In Massachusetts, in Virginia,
But we were England's, still colonials,
Possessing what we still were unpossessed by,
Possessed by what we now no more possessed.
Something we were withholding made us weak
Until we found out that it was ourselves
We were withholding from our land of living,
And forthwith found salvation in surrender.
Such as we were we gave ourselves outright
(The deed of gift was many deeds of war)
To the land vaguely realizing westward,
But still unstoried, artless, unenhanced,
Such as she was, such as she would become.

COME IN

As I came to the edge of the woods,
Thrush music—hark!
Now if it was dusk outside,
Inside it was dark.

Too dark in the woods for a bird
By sleight of wing
To better its perch for the night,
Though it still could sing.

The last of the light of the sun
That had died in the west
Still lived for one song more
In a thrush's breast.

Far in the pillared dark
Thrush music went—
Almost like a call to come in
To the dark and lament.

But no, I was out for stars:
I would not come in.
I meant not even if asked,
And I hadn't been.

FIREFLIES IN THE GARDEN

Here come real stars to fill the upper skies,
And here on earth come emulating flies,
That though they never equal stars in size,
(And they were never really stars at heart)
Achieve at times a very star-like start.
Only, of course, they can't sustain the part.

35

DEVOTION

The heart can think of no devotion
Greater than being shore to the ocean—
Holding the curve of one position,
Counting an endless repetition.

A PASSING GLIMPSE

I often see flowers from a passing car
That are gone before I can tell what they are.

I want to get out of the train and go back
To see what they were beside the track.

I name all the flowers I am sure they weren't:
Not fireweed loving where woods have burnt—

Not blue bells gracing a tunnel mouth—
Not lupine living on sand and drouth.

Was something brushed across my mind
That no one on earth will ever find?

Heaven gives its glimpses only to those
Not in position to look too close.

ONE GUESS

He has dust in his eyes and a fan for a wing,
A leg akimbo with which he can sing,
And a mouthful of dyestuff instead of a sting.

THE OVEN BIRD

There is a singer everyone has heard,
Loud, a mid-summer and a mid-wood bird,
Who makes the solid tree trunks sound again.
He says that leaves are old and that for flowers
Mid-summer is to spring as one to ten.
He says the early petal-fall is past
When pear and cherry bloom went down in showers
On sunny days a moment overcast;
And comes that other fall we name the fall.
He says the highway dust is over all.
The bird would cease and be as other birds
But that he knows in singing not to sing.
The question that he frames in all but words
Is what to make of a diminished thing.

39

A DRUMLIN WOODCHUCK

One thing has a shelving bank,
Another a rotting plank,
To give it cozier skies
And make up for its lack of size.

40

My own strategic retreat
Is where two rocks almost meet,
And still more secure and snug,
A two-door burrow I dug.

With those in mind at my back
I can sit forth exposed to attack
As one who shrewdly pretends
That he and the world are friends.

All we who prefer to live
Have a little whistle we give,
And flash, at the least alarm
We dive down under the farm.

We allow some time for guile
And don't come out for a while
Either to eat or drink.
We take occasion to think.

And if after the hunt goes past
And the double-barrelled blast
(Like war and pestilence
And the loss of common sense),

If I can with confidence say
That still for another day,
Or even another year,
I will be there for you, my dear,

It will be because, though small
As measured against the All,
I have been so instinctively thorough
About my crevice and burrow.

DEPARTMENTAL

An ant on the table cloth
Ran into a dormant moth
Of many times his size.
He showed not the least surprise.
His business wasn't with such.
He gave it scarcely a touch,
And was off on his duty run.
Yet if he encountered one
Of the hive's enquiry squad
Whose work is to find out God
And the nature of time and space,
He would put him onto the case.

43

Ants are a curious race;
One crossing with hurried tread
The body of one of their dead
Isn't given a moment's arrest—
Seems not even impressed.
But he no doubt reports to any
With whom he crosses antennae,
And they no doubt report
To the higher up at court.
Then word goes forth in Formic:
"Death's come to Jerry McCormic,
Our selfless forager Jerry.
Will the special Janizary
Whose office it is to bury
The dead of the commissary
Go bring him home to his people.

44

Lay him in state on a sepal.
Wrap him for shroud in a petal.
Embalm him with ichor of nettle.
This is the word of your Queen."
And presently on the scene
Appears a solemn mortician;
And taking formal position
With feelers calmly atwiddle,
Seizes the dead by the middle,
And heaving him high in air,
Carries him out of there.
No one stands round to stare.
It is nobody else's affair.

It couldn't be called ungentle.
But how thoroughly departmental.

CANIS MAJOR

The great Overdog,
That heavenly beast
With a star in one eye,
Gives a leap in the east.

He dances upright
All the way to the west
And never once drops
On his forefeet to rest.

I'm a poor underdog,
But tonight I will bark
With the great Overdog
That romps through the dark.

A MINOR BIRD

I have wished a bird would fly away,
And not sing by my house all day;

Have clapped my hands at him from the door
When it seemed as if I could bear no more.

The fault must partly have been in me.
The bird was not to blame for his key.

And of course there must be something wrong
In wanting to silence any song.

47

THE ROSE FAMILY

The rose is a rose,
And was always a rose.
But the theory now goes
That the apple's a rose,
And the pear is, and so's
The plum, I suppose.
The dear only knows
What will next prove a rose.
You, of course, are a rose—
But were always a rose.

THE SECRET SITS

We dance round in a ring and suppose,
But the Secret sits in the middle and knows.

48

THE PASTURE

I'm going out to clean the pasture spring;
I'll only stop to rake the leaves away
(And wait to watch the water clear, I may):
I shan't be gone long.—You come too.

I'm going out to fetch the little calf
That's standing by the mother. It's so young
It totters when she licks it with her tongue.
I shan't be gone long.—You come too.

THE ROAD NOT TAKEN

Two roads diverged in a yellow wood,
And sorry I could not travel both
And be one traveler, long I stood
And looked down one as far as I could
To where it bent in the undergrowth;

Then took the other, as just as fair,
And having perhaps the better claim,
Because it was grassy and wanted wear;
Though as for that, the passing there
Had worn them really about the same,

And both that morning equally lay
In leaves no step had trodden black.
Oh, I kept the first for another day!
Yet knowing how way leads on to way,
I doubted if I should ever come back.

I shall be telling this with a sigh
Somewhere ages and ages hence:
Two roads diverged in a wood, and I—
I took the one less traveled by,
And that has made all the difference.

GATHERING LEAVES

Spades take up leaves
No better than spoons,
And bags full of leaves
Are light as balloons.

I make a great noise
Of rustling all day
Like rabbit and deer
Running away.

But the mountains I raise
Elude my embrace,
Flowing over my arms
And into my face.

I may load and unload
Again and again
Till I fill the whole shed,
And what have I then?

Next to nothing for weight;
And since they grew duller
From contact with earth,
Next to nothing for color.

Next to nothing for use.
But a crop is a crop,
And who's to say where
The harvest shall stop?

NOW CLOSE THE WINDOWS

Now close the windows and hush all the fields;
   If the trees must, let them silently toss;
No bird is singing now, and if there is,
   Be it my loss.

It will be long ere the marshes resume,
   It will be long ere the earliest bird:
So close the windows and not hear the wind,
   But see all wind-stirred.

A LATE WALK

When I go up through the mowing field,
    The headless aftermath,
Smooth-laid like thatch with the heavy dew,
    Half closes the garden path.

And when I come to the garden ground,
    The whir of sober birds
Up from the tangle of withered weeds
    Is sadder than any words.

A tree beside the wall stands bare,
    But a leaf that lingered brown,
Disturbed, I doubt not, by my thought,
    Comes softly rattling down.

I end not far from my going forth,
    By picking the faded blue
Of the last remaining aster flower
    To carry again to you.

ACQUAINTED WITH THE NIGHT

I have been one acquainted with the night.
I have walked out in rain—and back in rain.
I have outwalked the furthest city light.

I have looked down the saddest city lane.
I have passed by the watchman on his beat
And dropped my eyes, unwilling to explain.

I have stood still and stopped the sound of feet
When far away an interrupted cry
Came over houses from another street,

But not to call me back or say good-bye;
And further still at an unearthly height,
One luminary clock against the sky

Proclaimed the time was neither wrong nor right.
I have been one acquainted with the night.

THE LAST WORD OF A BLUEBIRD

As told to a child

As I went out a Crow
In a low voice said, "Oh,
I was looking for you.
How do you do?
I just came to tell you
To tell Lesley (will you?)
That her little Bluebird
Wanted me to bring word
That the north wind last night
That made the stars bright
And made ice on the trough
Almost made him cough
His tail feathers off.

58

He just had to fly!
But he sent her Good-by,
And said to be good,
And wear her red hood,
And look for skunk tracks
In the snow with an ax—
And do everything!
And perhaps in the spring
He would come back and sing."

A PECK OF GOLD

Dust always blowing about the town,
Except when sea fog laid it down,
And I was one of the children told
Some of the blowing dust was gold.

All the dust the wind blew high
Appeared like gold in the sunset sky,
But I was one of the children told
Some of the dust was really gold.

Such was life in the Golden Gate:
Gold dusted all we drank and ate,
And I was one of the children told,
"We all must eat our peck of gold."

TREE AT MY WINDOW

Tree at my window, window tree,
My sash is lowered when night comes on;
But let there never be curtain drawn
Between you and me.

Vague dream-head lifted out of the ground,
And thing next most diffuse to cloud,
Not all your light tongues talking aloud
Could be profound.

But tree, I have seen you taken and tossed,
And if you have seen me when I slept,
You have seen me when I was taken and swept
And all but lost.

That day she put our heads together,
Fate had her imagination about her,
Your head so much concerned with outer,
Mine with inner, weather.

63

QUESTIONING FACES

The winter owl banked just in time to pass
And save herself from breaking window glass.
And her wings straining suddenly aspread
Caught color from the last of evening red
In a display of underdown and quill
To glassed-in children at the windowsill.

DUST OF SNOW

The way a crow
Shook down on me
The dust of snow
From a hemlock tree

Has given my heart
A change of mood
And saved some part
Of a day I had rued.

66

THE RUNAWAY

Once when the snow of the year was beginning to fall,
We stopped by a mountain pasture to say, "Whose colt?"
A little Morgan had one forefoot on the wall,
The other curled at his breast. He dipped his head
And snorted at us. And then he had to bolt.
We heard the miniature thunder where he fled,
And we saw him, or thought we saw him, dim and grey
Like a shadow against the curtain of falling flakes.
"I think the little fellow's afraid of the snow.
He isn't winter-broken. It isn't play
With the little fellow at all. He's running away.
I doubt if even his mother could tell him, 'Sakes,
It's only weather.' He'd think she didn't know!
Where is his mother? He can't be out alone."
And now he comes again with clatter of stone,
And mounts the wall again with whited eyes
And all his tail that isn't hair up straight.
He shudders his coat as if to throw off flies.
"Whoever it is that leaves him out so late,
When other creatures have gone to stall and bin,
Ought to be told to come and take him in."

FIRE AND ICE

Some say the world will end in fire,
Some say in ice.
From what I've tasted of desire
I hold with those who favor fire.
But if it had to perish twice,
I think I know enough of hate
To say that for destruction ice
Is also great
And would suffice.

70

LOOKING FOR A SUNSET BIRD IN WINTER

The west was getting out of gold,
The breath of air had died of cold,
When shoeing home across the white,
I thought I saw a bird alight.

In summer when I passed the place
I had to stop and lift my face;
A bird with an angelic gift
Was singing in it sweet and swift.

No bird was singing in it now.
A single leaf was on a bough,
And that was all there was to see
In going twice around the tree.

From my advantage on a hill
I judged that such a crystal chill
Was only adding frost to snow
As gilt to gold that wouldn't show.

A brush had left a crooked stroke
Of what was either cloud or smoke
From north to south across the blue;
A piercing little star was through.

73

STOPPING BY WOODS ON A SNOWY EVENING

Whose woods these are I think I know.
His house is in the village though;
He will not see me stopping here
To watch his woods fill up with snow.

My little horse must think it queer
To stop without a farmhouse near
Between the woods and frozen lake
The darkest evening of the year.

He gives his harness bells a shake
To ask if there is some mistake.
The only other sound's the sweep
Of easy wind and downy flake.

The woods are lovely, dark and deep.
But I have promises to keep,
And miles to go before I sleep,
And miles to go before I sleep.

74

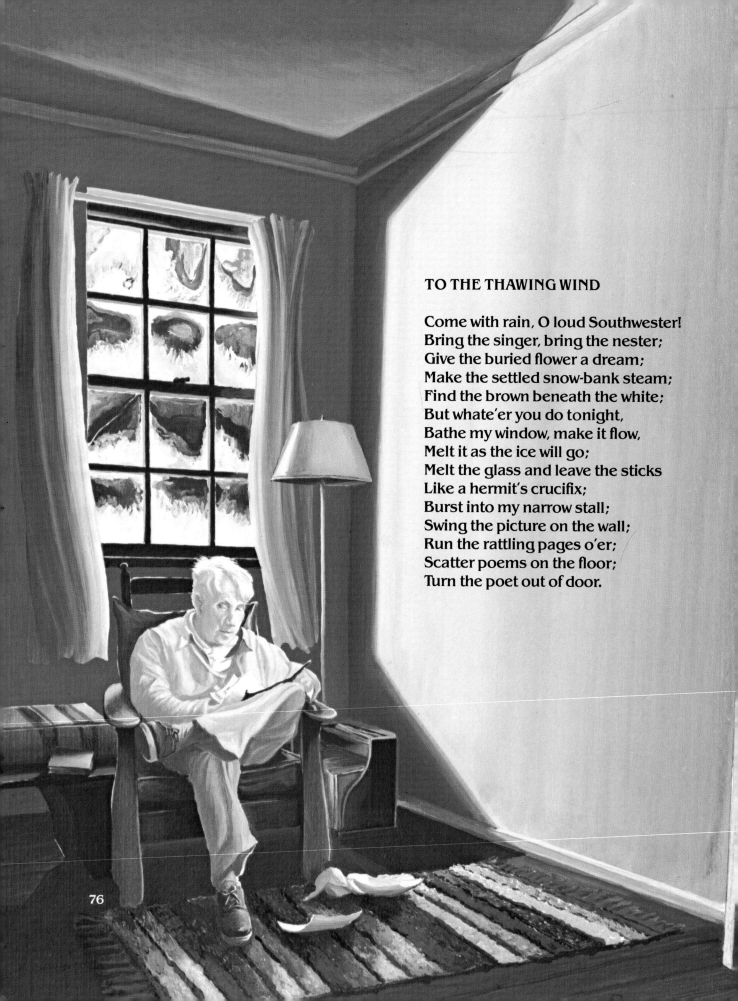

TO THE THAWING WIND

Come with rain, O loud Southwester!
Bring the singer, bring the nester;
Give the buried flower a dream;
Make the settled snow-bank steam;
Find the brown beneath the white;
But whate'er you do tonight,
Bathe my window, make it flow,
Melt it as the ice will go;
Melt the glass and leave the sticks
Like a hermit's crucifix;
Burst into my narrow stall;
Swing the picture on the wall;
Run the rattling pages o'er;
Scatter poems on the floor;
Turn the poet out of door.

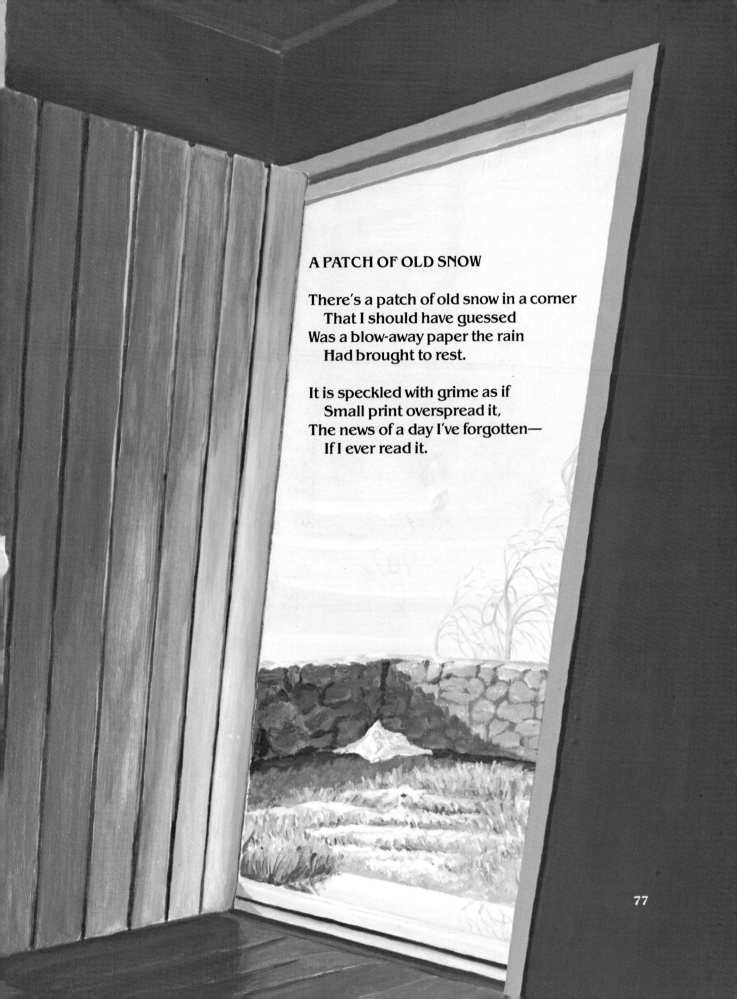

A PATCH OF OLD SNOW

There's a patch of old snow in a corner
    That I should have guessed
Was a blow-away paper the rain
    Had brought to rest.

It is speckled with grime as if
    Small print overspread it,
The news of a day I've forgotten—
    If I ever read it.

Glossary

aftermath a new growth of grass that comes after a field has been mowed one or more times. See *A Late Walk,* page 55.

avalanching sliding or rushing downward suddenly, as happens when great masses of snow are detached from a mountainside in an avalanche. See *Birches,* page 18.

bole the trunk of a tree. See *A Young Birch,* page 28.

bracken large ferns, or a place that is overgrown with ferns and scrubby shrubs. See *Birches,* page 18.

Canis Major the Great Dog constellation of stars which includes Sirius, the dog star, "in one eye" of "that heavenly beast," compared with the poet, "the poor underdog" of *Canis Major,* page 46.

commissary the unit that supplies food for large groups, such as an army or a corporate headquarters, or in *Departmental,* page 44, a hive of ants.

crazes cracks in a network pattern of thin lines, as happens sometimes in old glazed dishes or pottery, or when potters try deliberately for this effect. See *Birches,* page 18.

decayed rotted or decomposed; broken down into a form that mixes with the soil to produce good, nutritious compost for growing things. See *In Hardwood Groves,* page 27.

diffuse spread out thinly. See *Tree at My Window,* page 62.

diminished made less; in the case of *The Oven Bird,* page 39, changed for the worse.

diverged parted ways. See *The Road Not Taken,* page 51.

drumlin a long narrow ridge or hill, smoothly rounded, made in prehistoric times by a glacier pushing from behind. See *A Drumlin Woodchuck,* page 40.

elude avoid or escape. See *Gathering Leaves,* page 52.

Eden the fruit-and-flower-filled garden in which, according to the Biblical story, Adam and Eve first found themselves, living an idyllic existence until they were banished, after eating fruit from the Tree of Knowledge, and so causing their "grief." See *Nothing Gold Can Stay,* page 22.

emulating having the same appearance, or actually imitating. In the illustration for *Fireflies in the Garden,* page 35, the fireflies have managed to arrange themselves in the very same pattern as that of the constellation in the sky above them.

fireweed any of a number of weeds that take over areas of burned-out woodlands and thrive there. See *A Passing Glimpse,* page 37.

forager a scout and collector of necessary supplies; such as, in the case of *Departmental,* page 44, food supplies for the ants.

Formic	a word neatly made up by the poet to mean the language of ants, since anything related to ants is called "formic," derived from the Latin word for ant: *formica.* No connection with formic acid is intended although that useful liquid was originally made from ants, and so named for them. See *Departmental,* page 44.
Hyla	a genus of tree frogs; tiny creatures which sing melodiously by the thousands in spring, the mating season. See *Hyla Brook,* page 25.
ichor	usually the immortal fluid that was supposed to flow in the veins of the gods, but in the case of *Departmental,* page 45, a lovely word for nettle juice.
Janizary	usually a soldier in the Turkish army (sometimes spelled Janissary), but in *Departmental,* page 44, a special official.
Lesley	Robert Frost's daughter. See *The Last Word of a Bluebird,* page 58.
lichens	members of the fungus family, which come in shades of grey, green, yellow, brown, or black, and in a variety of leaflike, branchlike, or other shapes, and grow on rocks, trees, etc. See *Leaves Compared with Flowers,* page 26.
lupine	a plant with blue, pink or white flowers. See *A Passing Glimpse,* page 37.
luminary	light-giving or shining; in *Acquainted with the Night,* page 57, the image is that of the moon.
Morgan	Bred as light carriage and saddle horses, Morgans are descended from *Justin Morgan,* a stallion. See *The Runaway,* page 69.
peck	a measure; strictly defined, a dry measure of eight quarts, or one-quarter of a bushel. In *A Peck of Gold,* page 61, it more likely means just "a lot," as in "a peck of trouble."
pestilence	a contagious disease that spreads suddenly and uncontrollably; a plague. See *A Drumlin Woodchuck,* page 42.
pillared	filled with columns or pillars; but in *Come In,* page 32, great trees within the woods.
quill	one of the large feathers in the wing or tail of a bird. See *Questioning Faces,* page 64.
reminiscent	in a mood to recall memories; that is, to reminisce. See *A Young Birch,* page 28.
sash	the wooden frame of a window. See *Tree at My Window,* page 62.
shoeing	traveling on snowshoes. See *Looking for a Sunset Bird in Winter,* page 72.
trough	a large box full of water, from which horses or other livestock can drink. See *The Last Word of a Bluebird,* page 58.
underdown	the soft layer of plumage on the underside of a bird. See *Questioning Faces,* page 64.
wanted	lacked. See *The Road Not Taken,* page 50.

Designed by Barbara Holdridge

Composed in ITC Benguiat Book and Benguiat Medium
by Fototypesetters, Baltimore, Maryland

Color separation by Capper, Inc., Knoxville, Tennessee

Printed and bound in Hong Kong by
Everbest Printing Co., Ltd./Four Colour Imports, Ltd., Louisville, Kentucky